Leve
read lo
eager t

Speci

- Clear type
- Richer, more varied vocabulary
- Full, exciting story
- Longer sentences
- Detailed illustrations to capture the imagination

Educational Consultant: Geraldine Taylor
Book Banding Consultant: Kate Ruttle

A catalogue record for this book is available from the British Library

Published by Ladybird Books Ltd
80 Strand, London, WC2R 0RL
A Penguin Company

002
© LADYBIRD BOOKS LTD MMXIII
Ladybird, Read It Yourself and the Ladybird Logo are registered or unregistered trademarks of Ladybird Books Limited.

All rights reserved. No part of this publication may be reproduced, stored in a retrieval system, or transmitted in any form or by any means, electronic, mechanical, photocopying, recording or otherwise, without the prior consent of the copyright owner.

ISBN: 978-0-71819-476-5

Printed in China

Sam and the Robots

Written by Mandy Ross
Illustrated by Lisa Hunt

Sam was good at building things.
One day he built a robot.

"I'm Pod," said the robot.
"Who are you?"

"I'm Sam," said Sam.
"Pleased to meet you."

Pod the robot liked to build things, too.

"What shall we build now?" asked Sam one day.

"Can we build another robot, please?" said Pod.

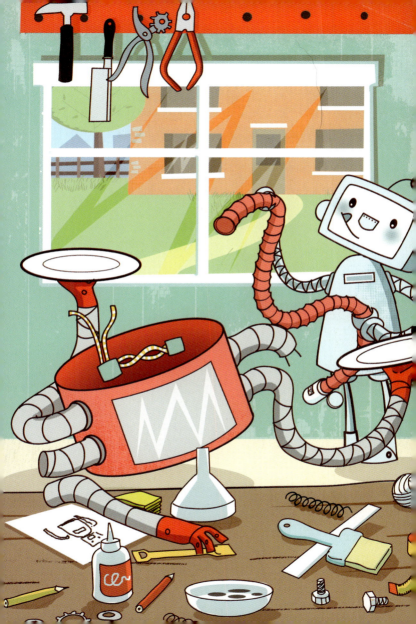

So Sam and Pod built a new robot. She was called Boots. Boots was a football robot and she was VERY good at her job. She scored goal after goal after goal.

Sam's school won the next match, and the next one. In fact, soon they had won ALL the football matches.

Sam and Pod built another new robot. He was called Dinner-Whizz. Dinner-Whizz was a robot who served school dinners.
Dinner-Whizz was VERY good at his job and served tasty school dinners on plate after plate.

Sam and Pod then built one more robot, called Chock. Chock was a robot who made yummy chocolates and he was also great at his job.

Everybody in the town wanted to eat Chock's tasty chocolates.

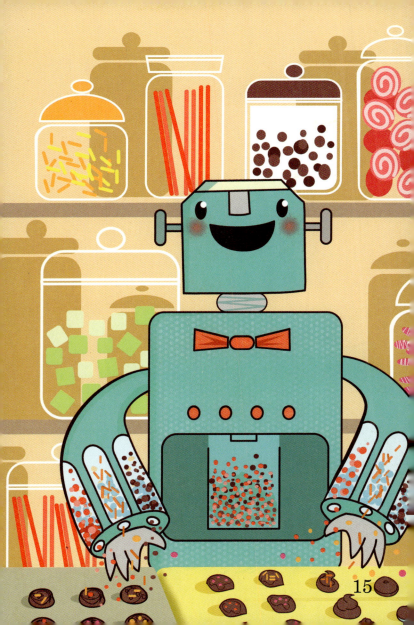

Sam and Pod kept on building new robots and soon the town was full of busy robots all working hard.

All day long, they swept and they mopped, and they mopped and they swept. The whole town was sparkling clean. Everybody was happy as nobody else needed to work at all.

One day though, it all went wrong. The robots had become too busy and they couldn't stop cleaning. "Stop!" said Sam.

But the robots just kept on working and working.

Boots scored ten goals... through ten windows at school.
CRASH! TINKLE!
"Stop, Boots!" cried Sam.

But Boots kept on scoring goals through one window after another.
CRASH! TINKLE!

Dinner-Whizz didn't stop serving school dinners, even though all the plates were full.
"Stop, Dinner-Whizz!" cried Sam.

But Dinner-Whizz kept on serving and soon the school was full of dinners.

Chock made all the wrong chocolates.
"Please stop, Chock!" cried Sam.
"Nobody wants chocolate carrots or chocolate pencils!"

But Chock would not stop.
He just kept on making the wrong chocolates. Soon, the whole town was full of chocolates.

Even Pod started to go wrong.
"I know what's wrong," said Sam.
"You robots need a holiday!"
"What's a holiday?" asked Pod.
"On a holiday, you have time to rest and have fun," said Sam.
"Yes please," said Pod. "As long as we can work, too…"

So Sam and the robots got on a train to the seaside.
"The train is fun – as long as we can still work," said Pod.

The robots started to work. They swept and they mopped, and they mopped and they swept. Soon, the whole train was sparkling clean.

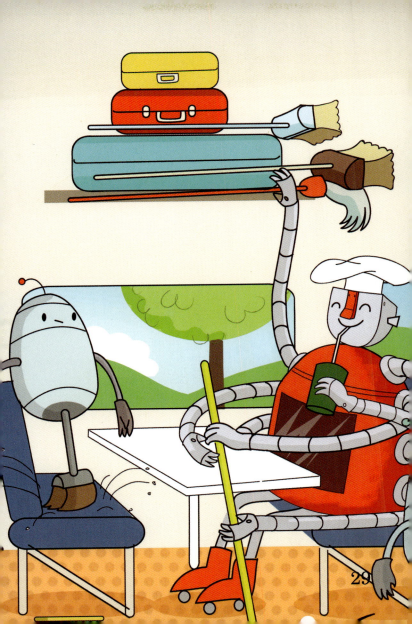

At last, the train got to the seaside. "Now we can rest and have some fun," said Sam. "The seaside does look fun!" said Pod. "All that sand needs sweeping away! All that water needs mopping up!"

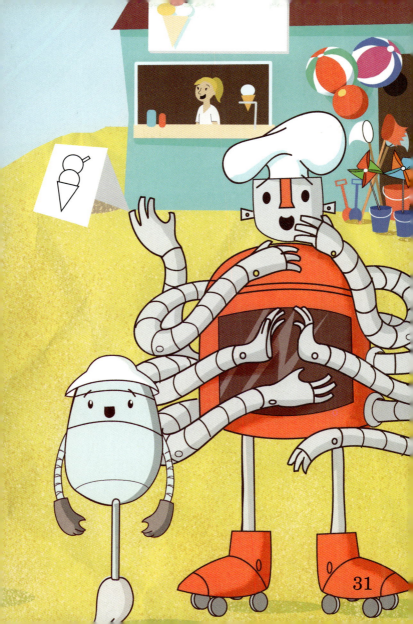

The robots started work. They swept at the sand, and they mopped up the water.

But the more they swept, the more sand there was. The more they mopped, the more water there was.

"No! Robots, please stop!" cried Sam. "You don't work on holiday! You have a rest in the sunshine, like this."

Sam lay down to have a rest. So then all the robots lay down, too.

But soon all the robots were bored. Pod and the others got up again. "Robots don't rest," said Pod. "We're bored. We need to be kept busy."

Then Sam had an idea. "I know what we need to do," he said.

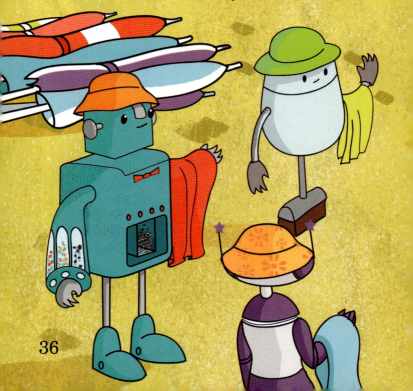

Sam, Pod and all the other robots got busy. They worked hard together in the sand. They dug and they built, and they built and they dug.

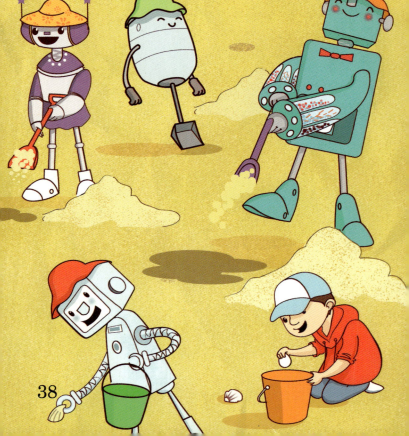

Sam and the robots built a big sandcastle. They kept on building all day long and the sandcastle got bigger and bigger and bigger!

"We've built a good sandcastle!" said the robots in the end.
"No," said Sam, "you've built a GREAT sandcastle!"

Then Sam said, "Now we'll all eat an ice cream."
"What's an ice cream?" asked Pod.
"It's a tasty, cold food," said Sam.
"No. We need cold, yummy oil, please," said Pod.
"Yes please, cold, yummy oil," said all the robots.

Sam and the robots got the last train back from the seaside.
"It was a great holiday," said Pod, "but we will be happy to get back home."
"And we will be VERY happy to get back to work!" said the other robots.

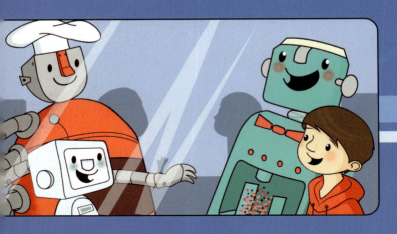

How much do you remember about the story of Sam and the Robots?
Answer these questions and find out!

- What is the name of the robot Sam builds first of all?

- What is Boots the robot very good at?

- Can you remember some of the wrong chocolates Chock makes?

- Where do Sam and the robots go on holiday?

- What do the robots do there?

- What do the robots have instead of ice cream?